The MAILBOX®
The Education Center®

WRITING Activity Cards
for EARLY FINISHERS

grades 4-6

76 Independent Activities

- ● **Writing skills tune-up**
- ● **Descriptive writing**
- ● **Personal narrative**
- ● **Imaginative narrative**
- ● **Expository writing**
- ● **Persuasive writing**

Just cut out and use!

Managing Editor: Sherry McGregor

Editorial Team: Becky S. Andrews, Diane Badden, Jacqueline A. Beaudry, Kimberley Bruck, Karen A. Brudnak, Pam Crane, Chris Curry, Colleen Dabney, Ann E. Fisher, Pierce Foster, Tazmen Hansen, Marsha Heim, Lori Z. Henry, Carol Lawrence, Debra Liverman, Kitty Lowrance, Amy Payne, Mark Rainey, Greg D. Rieves, Hope Rodgers, Rebecca Saunders, Donna K. Teal, Rachael Traylor, Sharon M. Tresino, Zane Williard

www.themailbox.com

Printed in China
10 9 8 7 6 5 4 3 2 1

903189001RRDSZ82010

Writing Activity Card Checklist

| Writing Tune-Up | 1 | 2 | 3 | 4 | 5 | 6 | 7 | 8 | 9 | 10 | 11 | 12 |

| Descriptive Writing | 13 | 14 | 15 | 16 | 17 | 18 | 19 | 20 | 21 | 22 |

| Personal Narrative | 23 | 24 | 25 | 26 | 27 | 28 | 29 | 30 | 31 | 32 | 33 | 34 | 35 | 36 |

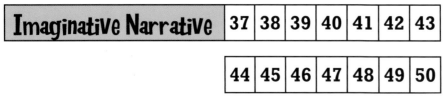

| Imaginative Narrative | 37 | 38 | 39 | 40 | 41 | 42 | 43 |
| | 44 | 45 | 46 | 47 | 48 | 49 | 50 |

Check or color the numbered space that matches your finished card.

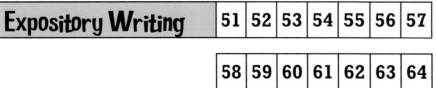

| Expository Writing | 51 | 52 | 53 | 54 | 55 | 56 | 57 |
| | 58 | 59 | 60 | 61 | 62 | 63 | 64 |

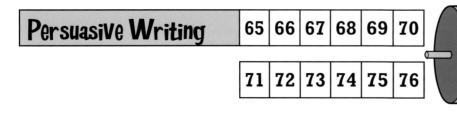

| Persuasive Writing | 65 | 66 | 67 | 68 | 69 | 70 |
| | 71 | 72 | 73 | 74 | 75 | 76 |

Note to the teacher: Have each child write his name on a copy of the page. Then have him check or color the numbered space of each activity card he finishes. Or use a copy of the page to track the cards you assign for independent work.

Table of Contents

Activity Cards for Early Finishers: Writing • ©The Mailbox® Books • TEC61326

Activity Cards for Early Finishers: Writing • ©The Mailbox® Books • TEC61326

Card	Skill
Personal Narrative	
23	Choosing a topic
24	Brainstorming
25	Developing a writing idea
26	Writing a strong lead
27	Organization, sequence
28	Sentence variety
29	Specific nouns and vivid adjectives
30	Strong verbs and adverbs
31	Elaboration: important details
32	Elaboration: sensory details
33	Voice
34	Writing for a specific audience
35	Writing a conclusion
36	Responding to a prompt

Card	Skill
Expository Writing	
51	Audience, purpose
52	Choosing a topic
53	Researching facts
54	Main idea
55	Important details, facts
56	Topic sentences
57	Organization
58	Organization
59	Transition words
60	Word choice
61	Sentence variety
62	Concluding sentences
63	Responding to a prompt
64	Responding to a prompt

Card	Skill
Persuasive Writing	
65	Audience, purpose
66	Stating an opinion
67	Supporting points
68	Supporting facts or examples
69	Examining other sides of an issue
70	Cause and effect
71	Introduction
72	Organization
73	Word choice
74	Conclusions
75	Responding to a prompt
76	Responding to a prompt

1 • Let's Get Specific

For each underlined word, write five specific nouns to replace it.

1. The zoo was crowded with <u>people</u>.
2. Mason took pictures of many <u>things</u>.
3. We saw some of the coolest <u>animals</u>.
4. My mom bought the yummiest <u>snack</u>.
5. We picked out <u>items</u> from the souvenir shop.

Challenge: Choose five nouns that start with different letters.

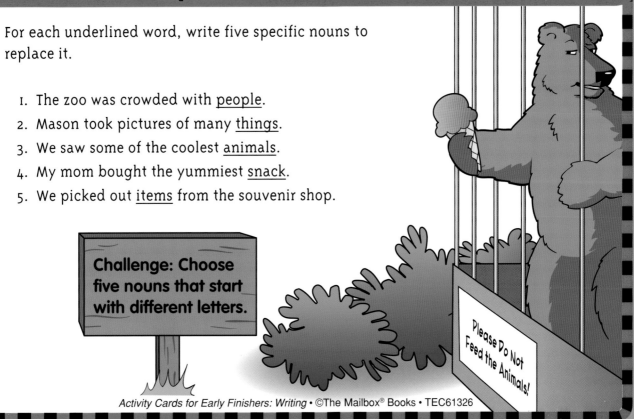

Please Do Not Feed the Animals!

Activity Cards for Early Finishers: Writing • ©The Mailbox® Books • TEC61326

---

2 • Heavy Weights

Rewrite each sentence twice, replacing the underlined word with a stronger verb each time.

1. Brutus, the weight lifter, <u>walked</u> onto the mat.
2. He <u>looked</u> at the enormous barbell.
3. The crowd watched Brutus <u>lift</u> the weight over his head.
4. The announcer <u>said</u> it was an excellent lift.
5. The judges <u>gave</u> Brutus his score.

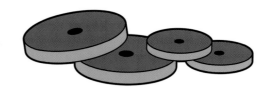

Activity Cards for Early Finishers: Writing • ©The Mailbox® Books • TEC61326

3 • It's a Party!

Copy the chart, making it larger than shown. Write at least one word or phrase in each box. Then write a paragraph describing one of the places.

Happy Birthday!

Surprise!

Place	See	Hear	Smell	Touch	Taste
movie theater					
amusement park					
birthday party					

Activity Cards for Early Finishers: Writing • ©The Mailbox® Books • TEC61326

4 • Shop 'til You Drop!

Where would you rather shop?

Plain Jane's Store

jeans

shoes

shirts

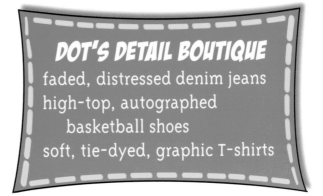

DOT'S DETAIL BOUTIQUE

faded, distressed denim jeans
high-top, autographed basketball shoes
soft, tie-dyed, graphic T-shirts

List five more items that could be sold in each store. Then choose one item in Dot's Detail Boutique. Write a paragraph to describe it.

Activity Cards for Early Finishers: Writing • ©The Mailbox® Books • TEC61326

Most of the sentences below follow the same pattern, which makes the paragraph dull to read. Rewrite the paragraph to make it more interesting.

Try using different types of sentences, changing the word order, and combining sentences.

The giant is very hungry. He wants some dinner. He wonders what he should eat. Then he decides to make his favorite dish, mashed potato and meat pie. He peels and cooks the potatoes. Then he chops the meat and vegetables. He bakes the pie. Finally, he eats.

Activity Cards for Early Finishers: Writing • ©The Mailbox® Books • TEC61326

Draw a staircase, like the one shown, on your paper. Choose a topic and plan a short story. Use a transition word in each step. Then write a one-page story.

Topics

- how I became world-famous in one hour
- how my little brother got stuck on a slide
- how a pencil saved my life
- how I earned my nickname
- how my mom survived her first camping trip

Activity Cards for Early Finishers: Writing • ©The Mailbox® Books • TEC61326

7 • It's Up for Discussion

Choose a topic and two characters from the chart.
Imagine what the characters might say about the topic.
Then write their dialogue.

I love the way the car responds to the controller, don't you?

Topics	Characters
least favorite foods	professional athlete
an exciting, new video game	school principal
a supercool amusement park ride	astronaut
	famous singer
riding a school bus	school nurse
driving a sports car	computer programmer

Mr. Apple said, "I love the way the car responds to the controller. Don't you?"

8 • She Knows It All!

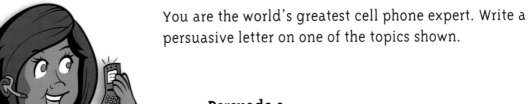

You are the world's greatest cell phone expert. Write a persuasive letter on one of the topics shown.

Persuade a

- movie director to use cell phones in more movie scenes

- high school student to buy a new cell phone

- retirement home to buy its residents cell phones instead of landline telephones

- store owner to feature the latest cell phone

9 • Critic's Corner

Pretend you are a food critic. Write eight similes that describe your favorite things to eat. Then write eight similes that describe your least favorite things to eat. Describe how each food looks, tastes, feels, smells, or even sounds when you eat it!

> **Remember!**
> A *simile* paints a picture for a reader.
> A *simile* makes a comparison by using the word *like* or *as*.

This spinach looks like slimy, green seaweed.

10 • Weather Report

Hint: In a *metaphor*, you describe one thing by comparing it to something very different, but don't use *like* or *as*.

The rain is a river running from the sky.

Complete each sentence using a metaphor.

1. The sunrise was...
2. Each clap of thunder is...
3. The raindrops fall in huge...
4. Pounding the roof, the hailstones are...
5. The sound of sleet hitting the sidewalk is...
6. The clouds rolling across the sky are...
7. Covering the sun, the rain cloud is...
8. The gust of wind is...
9. The sun's rays are...
10. When lightning flashes, it is...

What could you write about the topics shown on the pizza slices? For each one, choose a focus. Then write a topic sentence that names the topic and makes the focus clear. After that, choose one of your topic sentences and write a focused paragraph to go with it.

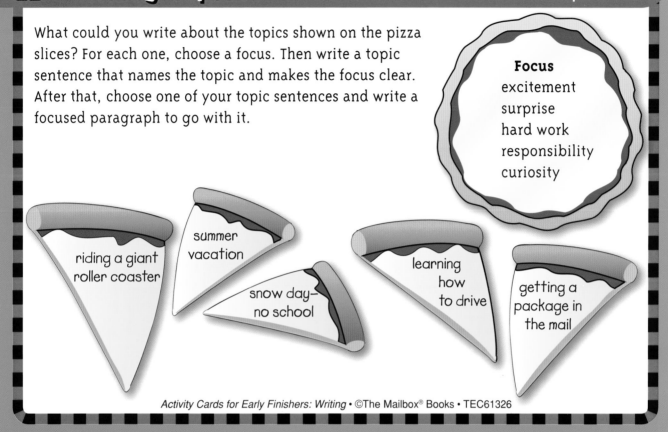

Focus
excitement
surprise
hard work
responsibility
curiosity

riding a giant roller coaster

summer vacation

snow day— no school

learning how to drive

getting a package in the mail

For each topic sentence, draw the organizer, making it larger than shown. Next, fill in each box with an important detail or a fact about the topic. Then choose one organizer and use it to write a five-sentence paragraph.

• Every child should have a robot that makes her bed.
• Anyone can learn to ride a bike.
• If you organize your desk, you may not lose anything.

topic sentence

1.

2.

3.

13 • I Aced It!

Think about the best day you have ever had at school. First, write an email to your best friend about the day. Then describe the day in a letter to your principal.

Don't forget to change your writing style to fit your audience and purpose. Use a friendly tone with other students and friends. Use a more formal tone with adults.

Activity Cards for Early Finishers: Writing • ©The Mailbox® Books • TEC61326

14 • What Am I?

Make your paper look like the one shown. Next, choose an object. Then complete the organizer with descriptive details about the object. Use your details to write a riddle similar to the one shown.

Riddle:
I am mostly hydrogen and helium. My light is white, but I look like a bright orange sphere. I reside millions of miles from Earth. It's a good thing I'm so far away because I put out a massive amount of heat, light, and energy. I hate to brag, but I am the center of the solar system. What am I?

Activity Cards for Early Finishers: Writing • ©The Mailbox® Books • TEC61326

Each topic sentence below should let the reader know what is going to be described. It should also make the reader want to read the description that follows. Rewrite each sentence. Then choose one and write the rest of the description.

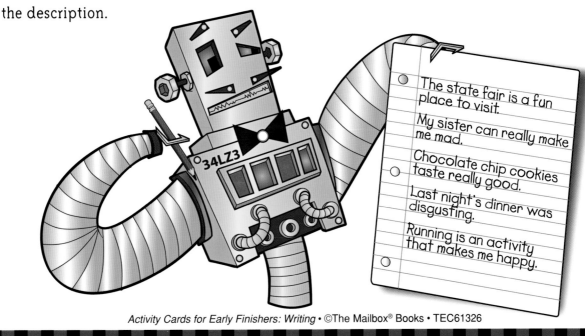

- The state fair is a fun place to visit.
- My sister can really make me mad.
- Chocolate chip cookies taste really good.
- Last night's dinner was disgusting.
- Running is an activity that makes me happy.

If you invented a video game, what would it be like? Draw the organizer shown and use it to brainstorm details about your game. Then use the details to describe your imaginary game.

Setting

Characters

Action

Goal

17 • Lost Crown Is Found!

Describe the recovery of the queen's crown for a local newspaper. Compare and contrast the event to finding a lost pet.

Ask yourself...

Where was the crown found?

How did the queen react?

What was the condition of the crown?

How was recovering the crown like or unlike finding a lost pet?

Activity Cards for Early Finishers: Writing • ©The Mailbox® Books • TEC61326

18 • What Are We Having?

Descriptive Writing
Developing a writing idea

Your best friend lost his or her glasses and cannot see anything clearly. Use your senses to describe the cafeteria lunch for him or her.

 Looks like:

 Sounds like:

 Smells like:

 Tastes like:

 Feels like:

Activity Cards for Early Finishers: Writing • ©The Mailbox® Books • TEC61326

Think of a supercool amusement park or water park ride.
Write a detailed description of the ride.

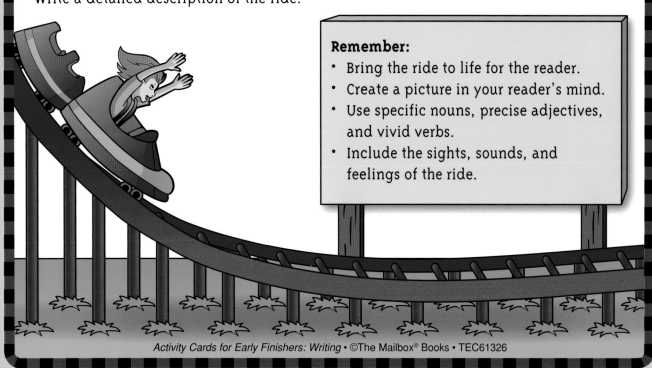

Remember:
- Bring the ride to life for the reader.
- Create a picture in your reader's mind.
- Use specific nouns, precise adjectives, and vivid verbs.
- Include the sights, sounds, and feelings of the ride.

The power is out. You need to get from your bed to the
bathroom. List five things you run into as you stumble
across your room. Then write a simile, metaphor, or
hyperbole to describe each item.

My stinky, old running shoes were speed bumps on my way out the door!

A *simile* compares two things using the word *like* or *as*.
A *metaphor* compares two different things without
  using the word *like* or *as*.
A *hyperbole* is a description that stretches the truth.

Draw a picture of the silliest hairstyle a teacher could have. Then write a paragraph to describe it. Next, circle all the nouns, verbs, adverbs, and adjectives. If a circled word is not precise, look it up in a thesaurus and replace it with a word that is.

Imagine you just had the best birthday party anyone could have. Describe it.

Respond to the prompt.
Include details for each of the categories shown.

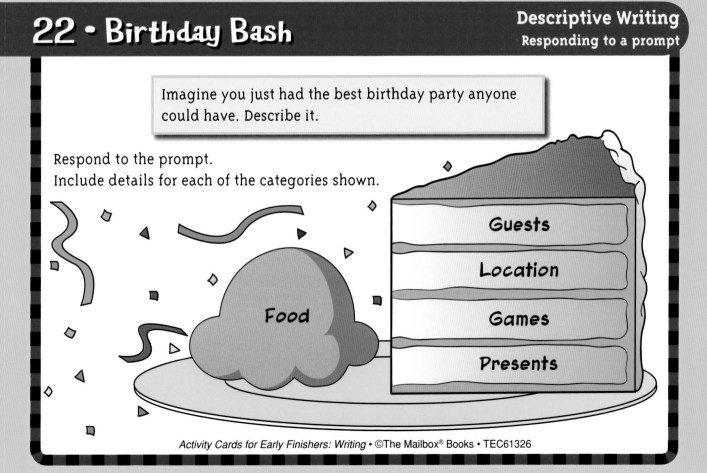

23 • On Target!

Choose an arrow with a prompt that reminds you of an unforgettable event. Then write a narrative about it.

Activity Cards for Early Finishers: Writing • ©The Mailbox® Books • TEC61326

24 • Idea Fireworks

Choose a topic from the firework. Then brainstorm details about the topic for each of the five Ws.

Activity Cards for Early Finishers: Writing • ©The Mailbox® Books • TEC61326

25 • Take It for a Spin!

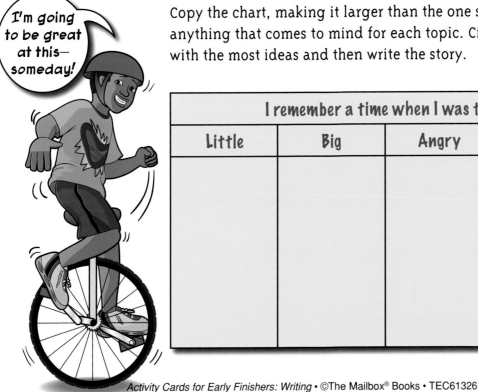

I'm going to be great at this—someday!

Copy the chart, making it larger than the one shown. Next, write anything that comes to mind for each topic. Circle the topic with the most ideas and then write the story.

I remember a time when I was too...			
Little	Big	Angry	Excited

Activity Cards for Early Finishers: Writing • ©The Mailbox® Books • TEC61326

26 • You Be the Judge

Number your paper 1–10. If a sentence is a strong lead, draw a check mark next to its number. If the sentence is not a strong lead, draw an X next to its number. Then rewrite each weak lead to make it a strong opening sentence.

America's Next Top Singer

To make your opening sentence strong, try starting with dialogue, an action, a question, or something funny!

1. My first thought that morning was "Oh no, not again!"
2. I sang my favorite song first because I like to sing it.
3. I auditioned Saturday morning.
4. Have you ever wanted something so bad you could taste it?
5. The audience clapped and clapped when I finished.
6. I was nervous about singing for the judges.
7. I sang so much that I couldn't even talk later.
8. The director called my name, and my legs turned to jelly.
9. "Good luck, honey!" was all I heard as I made my way onto the stage.
10. It was a day I will never forget.

Activity Cards for Early Finishers: Writing • ©The Mailbox® Books • TEC61326

27 • Ahoy, Matey!

Think about the most amazing place you've ever been. Next, make your paper look like the one shown. Then list details to describe your trip and tell each event in order.

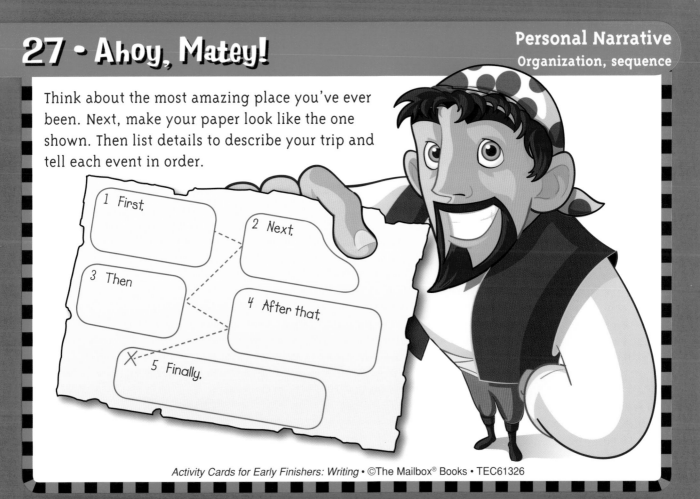

1 First,

2 Next,

3 Then

4 After that,

X 5 Finally,

28 • Jazz It Up!

Write about a time you made plans but they turned out differently. Was the change good or bad?

Keep your writing cool. Use different kinds and lengths of sentences.

TUNE-UP TIPS
- Make some sentences short and some sentences long.
- Use simple, compound, and complex sentences.
- Start a sentence with an introductory phrase that tells when, where, or why.
  - After dinner,...
  - Before the storm,...
  - Because I was hungry,...
  - In the cafeteria,...

29 • I Did It!

Think of a time you did something great you never thought you could do. Make a list of words that describe the event. Next, circle each noun on your list. Is it specific? If not, revise it. Then underline each adjective on your list. Is it vivid? If not, revise it. Then write about your experience. Choose words that help your reader experience the thrill of your accomplishment.

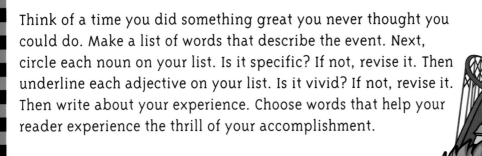

Nouns
not specific: ride, man, car
specific: roller coaster, Tower of Doom, neighbor, Mr. Johnson, mini van
Adjectives
not vivid: big, weird, fun, nice
vivid: gigantic, terrifying, exciting

30 • Front-Page News

You've been asked to write a newspaper article about a sporting event you either played in or attended. Since the article will not include a picture, your story needs to be rich in details. Use strong verbs to emphasize the action. Use adverbs to make it clear when, where, how, and how often something happened in the game.

Buzzer-Beating Shot Gracefully Swishes Through the Net

Strong Verbs
dash
sprint
stroll
struggle
dart
rush
bang
zip
aim
dribble
fling
toss
pitch
lob

Adverbs
wildly
gracefully
brilliantly
easily
well
backward
everywhere
immediately
suddenly
first
eventually

31 • To the Point!

Think about the last field trip you went on. Make your paper look like the one shown. List everything you did and everything that happened from the minute you arrived at school until the time you got back from the field trip. Next, circle the details that tell who, what, when, where, why, and how the field trip took place. Use the circled details to write a story about the trip.

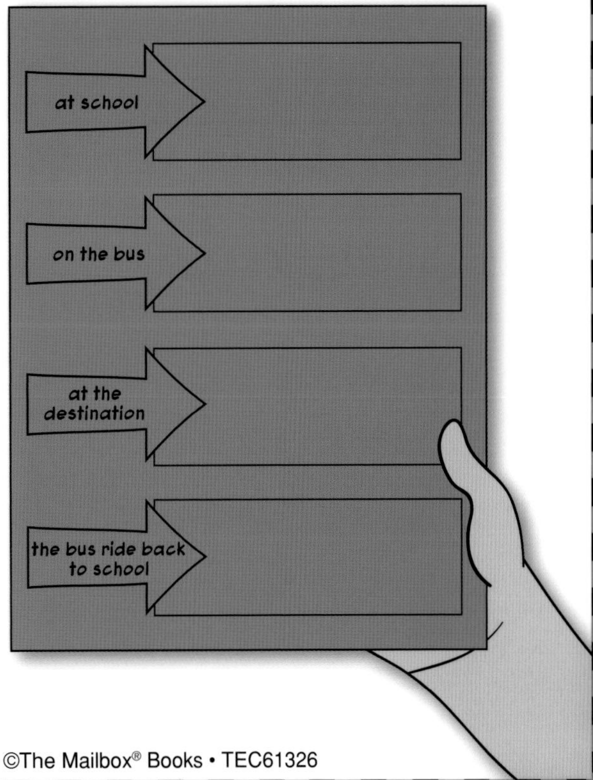

at school

on the bus

at the destination

the bus ride back to school

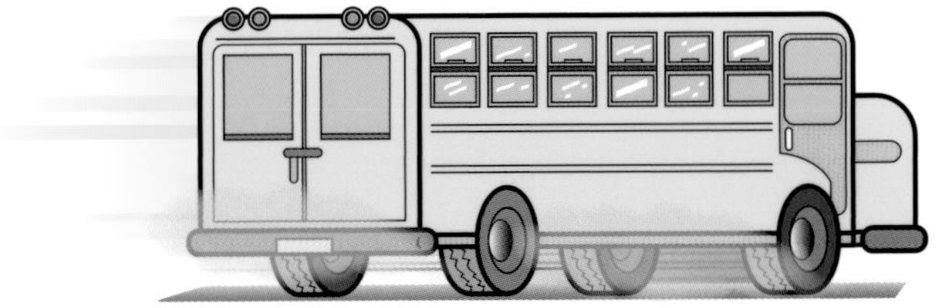

Activity Cards for Early Finishers: Writing • ©The Mailbox® Books • TEC61326

32 • Stretch It Out!

Think about a time when you were outside for a long time. List sensory details about the day. Then write a journal entry about it.

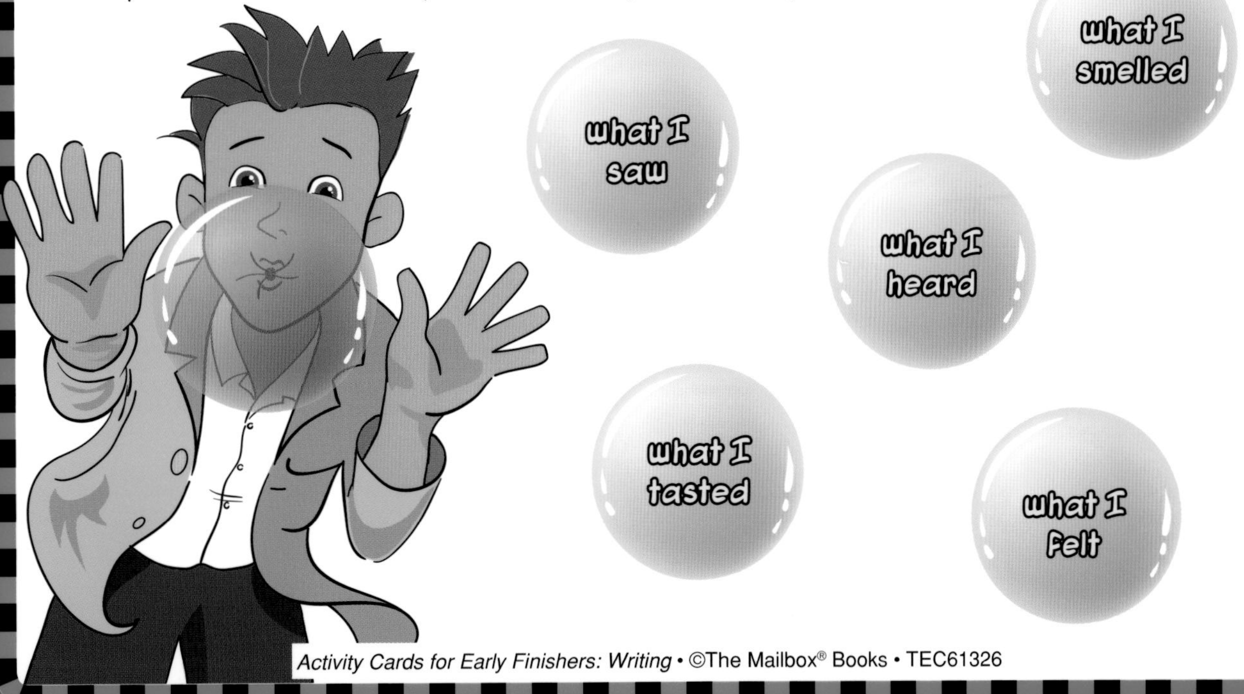

what I smelled

what I saw

what I heard

what I tasted

what I felt

Activity Cards for Early Finishers: Writing • ©The Mailbox® Books • TEC61326

33 • I Was Feeling...

Choose one of the moods below to describe how you felt on the first day of school this year. Brainstorm a list of words to help your reader feel your mood. Then write a paragraph about the first day, making sure the mood you've chosen shows in your writing.

Moods

cranky
hopeful
mischievous
sleepy
surprised

nervous
excited
worried
bouncy
cheerful

Activity Cards for Early Finishers: Writing • ©The Mailbox® Books • TEC61326

---

34 • It Wasn't Fair!

Think about a time when something happened that seemed very unfair. Answer the questions shown. Then write a letter to the person who was in charge. Describe the event so that person will understand your point of view.

Where were you?

What happened?

What do you think should have happened?

What did you do?

How did you feel?

Activity Cards for Early Finishers: Writing • ©The Mailbox® Books • TEC61326

35 • My Final Thought

A great conclusion leaves the reader with an interesting question or thought about your topic. Rewrite each dull ending to make it a great conclusion.

As the cake oozed off the plate, I decided I would not make up recipes anymore when I'm bored.

Topic: a story about an embarrassing moment

Dull ending: I was glad the day was over.

Topic: a story about how you learned an important lesson

Dull ending: That's the lesson I learned.

Topic: a story about being the guest of honor at a surprise party

Dull ending: It was a fun day.

Topic: a story about getting your first pet

Dull ending: That's how I met Bailey.

36 • Never Again!

I will never—and I mean never—eat another...

Respond to the prompt.
Write to entertain.

For each category shown, list information about yourself. Then list information for a main character you could write about. Give your character some characteristics that are similar to yours. Finally, write a paragraph that describes your character.

Challenges

Goals

Personality traits

Hobbies and interests

Likes and dislikes

38 • When and Where

Imaginative Narrative
Developing setting

The setting is when and where a story takes place. Choose a setting. List what a person might see, hear, touch, taste, and smell in the setting. Then use your list to write a story about an adventure that takes place in your setting.

Man, what is that delicious smell? Wait, it's coming to me... chocolate-chip pancakes! Dad's whistling off-key in the kitchen. I can hear the bacon sizzling....

Story Settings

- A dentist's office on a busy morning
- A shopping mall in December
- A Saturday morning at your house
- A movie theater during a scary movie

39 • Plot Pie

A story's plot is made up of events that happen as a character faces problems. Plan a story plot by answering the questions below.

Use your answers to write a story.

1 > **Beginning (Exposition):** What is the character's problem? What event starts the character's adventure?

2 > **Adventure (Rising Action):** Who does the character meet? What obstacles does he or she face?

3 > **The Big Event (Climax):** What is the most exciting part of the story?

4 > **Results (Falling Action):** What happens right after the climax? How are things starting to be wrapped up?

5 > **Wrap-Up (Resolution):** What loose ends are tied up? What rewards or punishments are given out?

Activity Cards for Early Finishers: Writing • ©The Mailbox® Books • TEC61326

40 • Ready...or Not?

Reggie the robot, the class's science fair project, is in pieces on the classroom floor. What happened? Draw the organizer on a large sheet of unlined paper. In the organizer's shapes, tell what you think happened to Reggie.

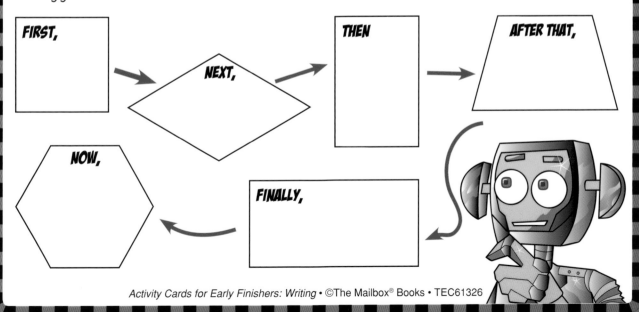

FIRST,   NEXT,   THEN   AFTER THAT,

NOW,   FINALLY,

Activity Cards for Early Finishers: Writing • ©The Mailbox® Books • TEC61326

41 • Two by Two

Chloe and Clare are excited about a special event. To plan a story about their time at the event, list important details about each topic below. When you finish, use your ideas to write a three-paragraph story about the girls' time at the event.

Activity Cards for Early Finishers: Writing • ©The Mailbox® Books • TEC61326

42 • Cafeteria Caper

Skeeter slipped into the cafeteria and snooped through the trash. Rewrite each of Skeeter's comments by adding at least one detail that would appeal to a reader's sense of touch, sight, smell, hearing, or taste.

1. Do I smell bacon?
2. Wow, it's a banana!
3. I got a whiff of something.
4. I like bread.
5. This looks like a banquet.
6. I'd like a drink.
7. That lunch bag is gross.
8. This package is hard to open.
9. Why did someone throw out this apple?
10. Is it time for dessert?

Activity Cards for Early Finishers: Writing • ©The Mailbox® Books • TEC61326

43 • Fast-Food Focus

Each piece of writing has a purpose: to entertain, to persuade, or to inform. Imagine you are one of the fast-food items below. Write a three-paragraph story on your item's topic. Be sure your story matches the purpose.

TO ENTERTAIN

A taco spices things up by sharing about its most embarrassing moment.

TO PERSUADE

A soda can tries to convince you that it should be recycled.

TO INFORM

A cheeseburger comments on why a diet of fast food isn't healthy.

Activity Cards for Early Finishers: Writing • ©The Mailbox® Books • TEC61326

---

44 • Very Different Voices

Choose one character pair below. Write a short letter from each character to the other, explaining his or her point of view. Be sure your reader can "hear" the differences between the two voices.

Yawn...

- A boy who wants to play with his dog
- The boy's dog, who just wants to sleep

- A college student who loves getting up early
- The student's roommate, who always goes to bed really late

- A teenager who likes to keep her room neat
- The teen's little sister, who loves playing with her big sister's stuff

Activity Cards for Early Finishers: Writing • ©The Mailbox® Books • TEC61326

Strong adverbs can help a story come alive. Pretend that you look out your classroom window and see something *very* strange raining from the sky. Use adverbs, such as those shown, to write a story about what happens next. Circle each adverb in your story and underline the verb it modifies.

often
greedily
swiftly
rarely
fiercely
mysteriously
outside
gently
soon
awkwardly

Activity Cards for Early Finishers: Writing • ©The Mailbox® Books • TEC61326

The owner of a local Chinese restaurant has donated a gigantic carton of fortune cookies for a class party. His only request is that the class write new fortunes for his next batch of cookies. Write 15 fortunes that each include at least one vivid adjective. Circle each adjective and underline the noun it describes.

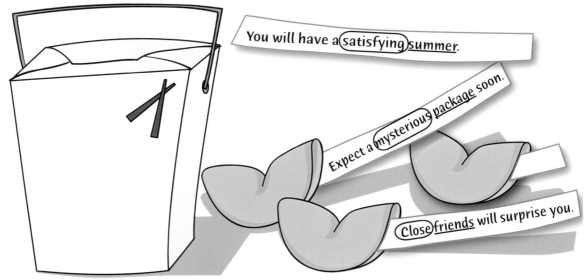

You will have a (satisfying) summer.

Expect a (mysterious) package soon.

(Close) friends will surprise you.

Activity Cards for Early Finishers: Writing • ©The Mailbox® Books • TEC61326

A good conclusion wraps up a story. One way to write a conclusion is to end with a question. Read the example. Then choose a story from below. Write a conclusion that wraps up the story and ends with a question.

What was I thinking?

Example: Goldilocks had never been more frightened in her life. She decided that it would be a very long time before she would eat someone's soup or sit in his chair without asking. Can you blame her?

- *Little Red Riding Hood*
- *Jack and the Bean Stalk*
- *The Three Little Pigs*
- *The Three Billy Goats Gruff*

One way to wrap up a story is to hint at the beginning of a new story. Read the example. Then choose a tale from below. Write a conclusion that wraps up the story and hints at the start of a new one.

Grizzly Glue

Example: The bears repaired Baby Bear's broken chair and cleaned up the porridge dishes. As they worked, they wondered about Goldilocks. Little did they know that Goldilocks was thinking too, planning her next visit to the bears' house.

- *Little Red Riding Hood*
- *Jack and the Bean Stalk*
- *The Three Little Pigs*
- *The Three Billy Goats Gruff*

49 • What's for Dinner?

It's Friday, and your two best friends are spending the night. Your mom yells, "Dinner is ready!" Then she brings out the weirdest food you've ever seen. Write a short story about this unusual meal.

Respond to the prompt. Start your story with this sentence:

When my mom told my friends and me what was for dinner, we couldn't believe it!

Activity Cards for Early Finishers: Writing • ©The Mailbox® Books • TEC61326

---

50 • Field Trip of Dreams

Field trips are fun and exciting, aren't they? What is the most unusual field trip you can imagine? Write a short story about going on this field trip with your class.

Respond to the prompt. Start your story with this sentence:

I never thought in a gazillion years that we'd go <u>there</u> for a field trip!

Activity Cards for Early Finishers: Writing • ©The Mailbox® Books • TEC61326

51 • These Are the Shoes

Your company is introducing a new athletic shoe. Your job is to inform others about this shoe. Write a paragraph that presents the shoe to parents. Then write a second paragraph that introduces the shoe to kids. Use the tips to help you.

Tips

- The purpose of your paragraphs is to inform. Don't try to convince someone to buy the shoe; just tell each audience about the shoe.

- Remember each paragraph's audience. Parents are concerned about cost and quality. Kids want a shoe that's cool, feels good, and looks great.

---

52 • Too Big!

When you write a report, you need to choose a writing topic that isn't too big or general (for example, "food" or "cars"). Instead, choose a specific topic, such as "The History of Pizza" or "Henry Ford's First Car." Write two specific writing topics for each too-big topic below.

Downsize it, dude!

Too-Big Topics

- Sports
- Education
- Food
- Animals
- Cars
- Music
- Hobbies
- Jobs
- Cities
- Memories

53 • Line Up!

One way to research facts for an expository essay is to make a line diagram. Look at the sample line diagram. Then choose a topic below. Research the topic and complete a line diagram on it.

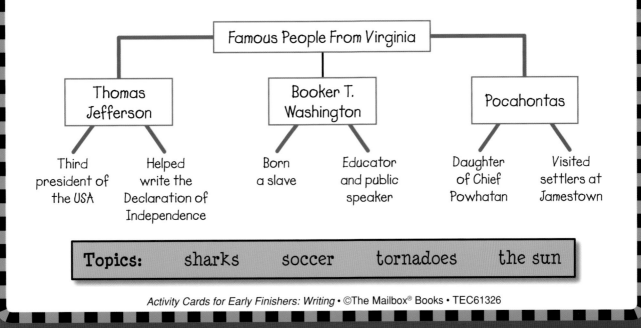

| Topics: | sharks | soccer | tornadoes | the sun |

Activity Cards for Early Finishers: Writing • ©The Mailbox® Books • TEC61326

---

54 • The "Mane" Thing

The main idea of an expository paragraph or essay is the most important point the writer wants the reader to know about the topic. For each topic, write a main idea you could write a paragraph about.

Lions are very brave creatures. They...

EXAMPLE
Topic: snakes
Main idea: Not all snakes are venomous.

1. **cheese pizza**
2. **my favorite game**
3. **field trips**
4. **bullying**
5. **my town**
6. **my bedroom**

Now chose one topic and main idea. Write a paragraph that includes your main idea, three supporting details, and a concluding sentence.

Activity Cards for Early Finishers: Writing • ©The Mailbox® Books • TEC61326

55 • Too Scary for Words

The purpose of expository writing is to inform or explain something to the reader. A newspaper is featuring an article on scary movies. The editor wants you to contribute to the article. Write a paragraph that explains why you do or do not like scary movies.

Tips

- State the main idea in the first sentence.

- Include at least three details or reasons that support your main idea.

- Finish the paragraph with a concluding sentence that restates your main idea in different words.

I can't look!

I can!

Activity Cards for Early Finishers: Writing • ©The Mailbox® Books • TEC61326

---

56 • Topic Time

The topic sentence tells readers what your paragraph is about. A simple way to write a topic sentence is to use this formula:

Subject (Who or what?) **+ Focus** (What about him, her, or it?) **= Topic Sentence**
Sample topic sentence: Babysitting *(subject)* can be a very challenging job *(focus)*.

Copy and complete the chart.

Subject	Focus	Topic Sentence
movies		
exercise		
pets		
my neighborhood		
shopping		

Activity Cards for Early Finishers: Writing • ©The Mailbox® Books • TEC61326

57 • Alike and Different

One way to organize an expository essay is to *compare* (write about similarities) and *contrast* (write about differences) topics. Choose a pair of topics below. Write one paragraph that compares the two items. Then write a second paragraph that contrasts them.

Oops!

- soccer and basketball
- sneakers and high heels
- pizza and pancakes
- your classroom and your bedroom
- recycling trash and saving money
- bullying and robbery
- love and sunshine

58 • Mapping Out a Monday

Your class will have a substitute teacher next Monday. This teacher needs to know what an average Monday is like in your classroom. Use the outline to write a five-paragraph essay. Don't forget to organize the events in the correct sequence.

♥2 Sub!

A Monday in My Class

1. Introduction
2. Arrival time
3. Instructional time (the time between arrival and dismissal)
4. Dismissal time
5. Conclusion

59 • In the Meantime

Revise the sentences, using transitions to write a smooth-flowing paragraph.

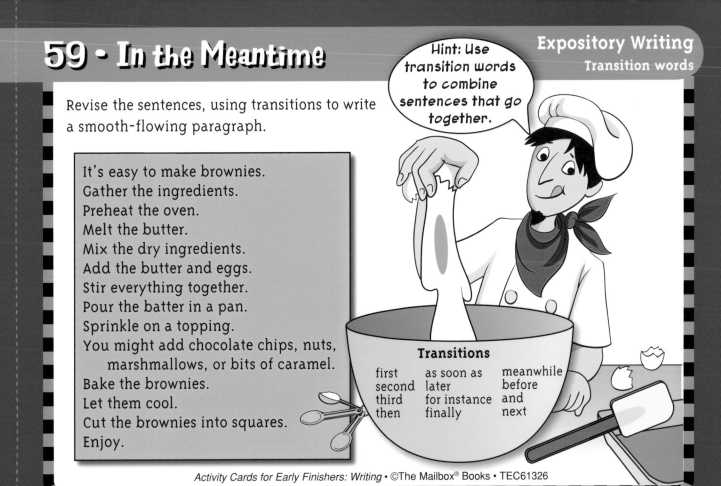

It's easy to make brownies.
Gather the ingredients.
Preheat the oven.
Melt the butter.
Mix the dry ingredients.
Add the butter and eggs.
Stir everything together.
Pour the batter in a pan.
Sprinkle on a topping.
You might add chocolate chips, nuts, marshmallows, or bits of caramel.
Bake the brownies.
Let them cool.
Cut the brownies into squares.
Enjoy.

Hint: Use transition words to combine sentences that go together.

Transitions

first	as soon as	meanwhile
second	later	before
third	for instance	and
then	finally	next

Activity Cards for Early Finishers: Writing • ©The Mailbox® Books • TEC61326

60 • A Masterpiece

An artist captures your attention and sense of whimsy with pictures. As a writer, you can take hold of your readers' attention with careful word choices. Choose one of the messy foods below. Then write a paragraph explaining the best way to eat it. Use words that will grab your readers' attention.

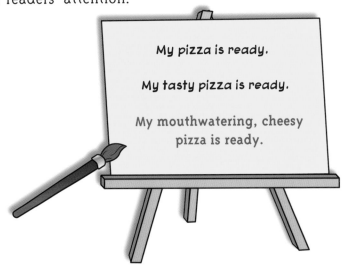

Messy Foods
- hot, mouthwatering, cheesy pizza
- ripe, juicy watermelon
- extrathick peanut butter and jelly sandwich
- double-decker ice cream cone
- slippery, saucy spaghetti
- drippy, overstuffed tacos

My pizza is ready.

My tasty pizza is ready.

My mouthwatering, cheesy pizza is ready.

Activity Cards for Early Finishers: Writing • ©The Mailbox® Books • TEC61326

61 • "Wand-erful" Revisions

The sentences in the paragraph below are boring. Rewrite the paragraph so there are different kinds and lengths of sentences.

A magician is not really magical. A magician is a performer. A magician does tricks for his or her audience. Most magicians do five basic kinds of magic tricks. Some magicians do close-up magic. A magician may seem to pull a coin out of a person's ear. Some magicians do escape magic. They seem to be able to escape from anything. Some magicians do illusions. They may make objects, animals, or people disappear. Some magicians do mentalist magic. They seem to read people's minds. Finally, some magicians do sleight of hand. They use skillful hand movements to amaze their audiences.

62 • That's All, Folks!

Make your paper look like the one shown. Next, find the concluding sentences for ten different paragraphs in a textbook. Write each one on your chart in the column that describes it. Then rank the sentences from 1 to 10, with 1 being the best concluding sentence.

Restates the Paragraph's Topic Sentence	Leads to the Next Paragraph	Emphasizes the Paragraph's Main Point	Rank

Imagine that your elderly neighbor has asked you to teach him how to text. He wants to be able to text his 15 grandchildren. How would you teach him to text?

Respond to the prompt.
Write a how-to essay that will help your neighbor learn how to text.

Start by listing each step. Next, explain each step. Then test your directions before writing your final copy.

Imagine you have been asked to be your school's ambassador. It will be your job to give tours of the school. Write the speech you will use as you guide visitors around your school.

Respond to the prompt. Write a speech you could read that points out the most important and interesting elements of your school.

To your left,...

65 • Meat Loaf Monday

Your principal has just instituted Meat Loaf Monday. Write an email to convince her this is a bad idea. Copy the organizer shown. Name three reasons Meat Loaf Monday is a bad idea. Then list supporting details for each reason.

Is the meat loaf supposed to be green?

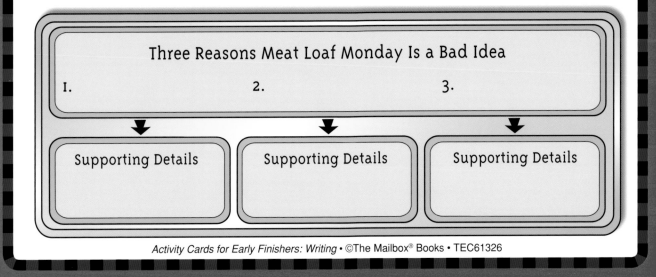

Three Reasons Meat Loaf Monday Is a Bad Idea

1.   2.   3.

| Supporting Details | Supporting Details | Supporting Details |

66 • Tell Me Why

Copy and complete each sentence. Then choose one sentence and write a paragraph that will persuade your readers to agree.

Think of two points that support your opinion. Explain those points in your paragraph.

1. I should be allowed to…
2. I wish everyone…
3. The best thing to eat for breakfast is…
4. Every classroom should have…

67 • Canine Clothing?

Should dogs wear clothes? Choose one of the opinions shown. Copy its points and write an example that supports each one. Then choose one point from the opposite opinion and describe a reason you disagree with it. Finally, use your ideas to write a persuasive article that clearly expresses your opinion.

Yes!
✓ Clothes make dogs look cute.
✓ Clothes make dogs feel loved and pampered.
✓ Clothes keep dogs warm and dry.

No!
X Clothes make dogs look silly.
X Clothes make dogs feel uncomfortable.
X Dogs already have fur, so clothes make them feel too warm.

Activity Cards for Early Finishers: Writing • ©The Mailbox® Books • TEC61326

68 • Count the Days

What do you think about going to school for four days a week instead of five? (For a four-day school week, you would probably be in school one hour longer each day.) Draw four boxes. In the first box, write a topic sentence that states your opinion. In the next three boxes, describe three reasons others should listen to you. Finally, create a persuasive poster that expresses your opinion.

R U for Four-Day Weeks?

Reason 1

Reason 2

Reason 3

Activity Cards for Early Finishers: Writing • ©The Mailbox® Books • TEC61326

Choose an issue from the list. Then draw a Venn diagram labeled as shown. Complete the diagram with reasons for both points of view.

Issue

- You want a cell phone with unlimited texting, but your mom says it's not worth the cost.

- You think chewing gum in class will help you be a better student, but the principal does not agree.

- Your best friend comes over. You want to play a video game, but your best friend wants to watch a movie.

- It's fast-food night at your house. You want pizza, but your sister wants tacos.

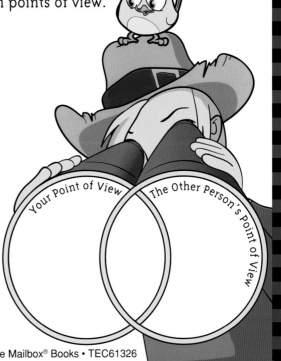

Your Point of View

The Other Person's Point of View

Activity Cards for Early Finishers: Writing • ©The Mailbox® Books • TEC61326

---

70 • Pricey Popcorn

At Center-City Cinema, the moviegoers have stopped buying popcorn. What might happen if the popcorn cost half as much as it used to? List three effects lower-priced popcorn could have on the theater's popcorn sales. Then write a letter to Mr. Moneybags, the owner of the theater. Convince him that lowering popcorn prices will be good for business.

Bag
~~$4.50~~ $2.25

Bucket
~~$6.50~~ $3.25

Tub
~~$7.50~~ $3.75

Activity Cards for Early Finishers: Writing • ©The Mailbox® Books • TEC61326

71 • That's a Stretch!

The paragraph shown is the introductory paragraph for a letter to a bubble gum company. It is not persuasive. Rewrite the paragraph so the reader will be eager to read the rest of the letter.

> To whom it may concern:
> Grape is the best flavor of gum. It makes the best bubbles. You should agree with me. No other flavor is better than grape.

Tips:
1. Try to grab the reader's attention by asking a question or expressing strong feelings in the first sentence.
2. Introduce the topic and your opinion.
3. Clearly state each supporting reason.

---

72 • Grand-Prize Surprise

You have entered a poster contest. Your poster is in the semifinals with four other posters. To win, you must write an email to the contest officials that will persuade them to choose your poster for the grand prize. Write a persuasive email to the officials using the format shown.

Persuasive Email Format

1st Paragraph: Write an introduction. Tell the contest officials what you want them to do and why.

2nd Paragraph: Write about a reason your poster should win the grand prize—"You should choose my poster because…"

3rd Paragraph: Write about another reason your poster should win the grand prize—"If you choose my poster…"

4th Paragraph: Give the reason no one else's poster should be chosen—"If you choose another poster…"

5th Paragraph: Write a conclusion. Creatively restate your main point. Then briefly review the reasons the officials should choose your poster.

73 • Dear Grandma,

Edit the letter to make it more interesting and persuasive. Use a thesaurus to add more powerful verbs, specific nouns, and vivid adjectives and adverbs.

Dear Grandma,
    My birthday is soon. Please do not send another puppy sweater this year. I am too old to wear something with puppies on it. I would like a gift card instead.
    None of the other kids my age wear puppy sweaters. They wear clothes with stripes or words on them.
    Now that I am older, I would like to buy my own clothes. It would really make me happy if you would just send a gift card.

Love,
Patrick

Activity Cards for Early Finishers: Writing • ©The Mailbox® Books • TEC61326

74 • Not Quite Right

Read the letter.
Then write a concluding paragraph.

Dear Top-Secret Kid's Room Cleaning Company President,

    Last week, the mess in my bedroom was out of control. My parents began to complain. So I decided to call your company to help me clean. I was not pleased with the work the crew did, and I want a refund.
    First of all, the cleaning crew arrived 30 minutes late. This upset me because my parents kept asking when my room was going to be clean. They almost grounded me because it was taking too long.
    Then, when the cleaning crew finally arrived, the cleaners just swept my dirty clothes under the bed. They stuffed all my things in the closet. This is not what I paid for them to do. I could have done that!

Activity Cards for Early Finishers: Writing • ©The Mailbox® Books • TEC61326

Imagine you want to watch your favorite television show or movie, but your family wants to watch something you think is boring. Write a speech that will convince them to watch your favorite show or movie instead.

Respond to the prompt.
In your speech, list three reasons your favorite show or movie is the better choice.

Trust me; you'll like my show much better!

Why?

Imagine that the latest trend at school is to call a calculator a *zigbot*. Do you think this is a good idea? Write a letter to the editor of your local newspaper to share your opinion about the trend and to convince readers to agree with you.

Respond to the prompt.
Write to persuade.

Where's my zigbot?!

Hint: Write an introductory sentence that introduces the topic and states your opinion. Next, describe at least two reasons for your opinion. Then restate your opinion in your conclusion.